Bleu Bleu gris

YVES SAINT LAURENT'S
STUDIO
MIRROR AND SECRETS

"The master, with
deft twists of hands
I could see were both
strong and delicate,
made an instant
sonnet of it."

Anthony Burgess

Yves Saint Laurent and his model Kirat in a butterfly print chiffon veil
for the autumn-winter 1977 haute couture collection.
Between look and mirror, Yves Saint Laurent's mystery.
Photograph André Perlstein

Cover: Yves Saint Laurent's glasses photographed by Hedi Slimane,
November 2008.

Unless otherwise indicated, all the quotations in bold are taken
from the writings of Yves Saint Laurent or answers given by him
in interviews.

© Actes Sud/Fondation Pierre Bergé - Yves Saint Laurent, 2014.
ISBN 978-2-330-03411-5
www.actes-sud.fr

Jéromine Savignon

Yves Saint Laurent's Studio

Mirror and Secrets

ACTES SUD
FONDATION PIERRE BERGÉ - YVES SAINT LAURENT

They say fashion has secrets? That if you find them, you can become a couturier? I'm not so sure. I prefer to speak of mysteries. Secrets can be passed on, but mysteries must be revealed.

In the studio where Yves Saint Laurent constructed his Oeuvre, I saw him battling the rebel forces that assailed him and emerge victorious. For forty years, I observed the ceremonial so eloquently described in this book: the drawing, the toile, the fitting, the fabric, the fitting, fitting again, the distribution of accessories. And, just as the chrysalis turns into a butterfly, so drawing gives rise to a garment. The mystery is tamed.

The mirror that covers a whole wall of the studio has always played an important role. It reflects and allows for reflection. We all want to know what's on the other side, to encounter the invisible, to pierce its mystery.

The studio is the heart of a couture house. It irrigates all the rest. We wanted to keep it just as Yves Saint Laurent left it. Here, time has stopped. His table, his chair and his white coat seem to be awaiting his return. We know that he will not be coming back, but sometimes, if we listen carefully, we can hear that heart, hear it beating.

Pierre Bergé

"Every artwork worthy of the name is a drama of the passions, if only because of the struggle between matter and the man taming it."

Jean Cocteau

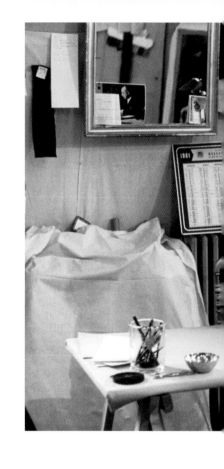

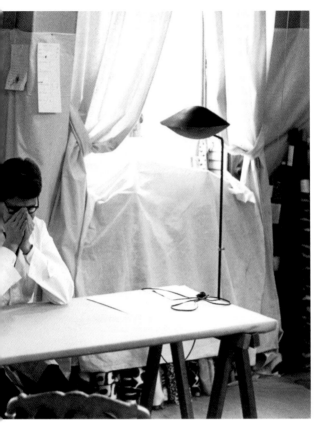

"I think that creators react to suffering
in the same way as they would resist
death, replacing immortality with art."

Anxiety and doubt: Yves Saint Laurent in his studio,
Rue Jean-Goujon, December 1961.
Photograph Pierre Boulat

Ludwig of Bavaria's Wagnerian labyrinths, the abyssal chaos of Francis Bacon's studio, the crystal belvedere of Hauteville House, home of the exiled Victor Hugo: these are the kind of potent places, saturated in emotions and secret passions that hold us spellbound, flooring us with "the shock of beauty"[1] delivered by their strange power. The power to escape from the showcase of souvenirs and into the intimate truth of human beings and objects. Yves Saint Laurent's studio is this kind of place.

But we barely have an inkling of this when, opening the heavy glass door at 5 Avenue Marceau, we enter the mansion occupied by the couture house from its apogee onwards, and afterwards by the Fondation Pierre Bergé - Yves Saint Laurent, that fathomless sanctuary of the Oeuvre and Myth that is "YSL".

1. John Ruskin.

A theatrical double row of kentias palms framing the short staircase leading to the salons, luxuriously soft-silent carpet in moiré Veronese green spreading all the way to the extremities of a very private first floor, Napoleon III wooden panelling, trompe l'oeil marble and mirrors fitted like "indiscreet jewels" to multiply the glitter of crystal chandeliers, long curtains in emerald velvet, padded sofas and screens with baroque gold fringes, statues of bacchantes and couture chairs. The atmosphere is Viscontian (the violence and passion of *Conversation Piece*), but also moves between the salon of Princess Mathilde and the boudoir of the Duchesse de Guermantes – or perhaps an opera set for Maria Callas in *La Traviata*. It is as if all the ceremonial splendours of the House of Dior have been filigreed into this interior, a bit like an ex-voto unconsciously dedicated to the man who was the first *maître à penser* in matters of couture to the very young Yves Mathieu-Saint-Laurent.

Yes, this is Saint Laurent's *Maison*, the original: not a copy, but like a slumbering belle touched by the magic wand of the fairy in *Sleeping Beauty*. Set out in a kind of endless 3-D freeze-frame, we could imagine her having escaped to the Pantheon of the fashion legend, never to return, leaving us, to remember her by, the sumptuous and faithfully preserved setting conceived for her by Yves Saint Laurent and Pierre Bergé. And this strange impression of coming to the couture house via a museum continues when, having climbed the thirty steps of the main staircase, and walked the long corridor at the top, we venture to open this door soberly marked with a single word: STUDIO. Now, another world opens, the "zone where the artist is king".[1]

After the sheer opulence of a residence made for La Castiglione comes the stunning contrast of a composition in beige and white, a pared-down functional interior of "unreal realism".[2] The room is spacious, deep, intimate. The curtains in simple couture cloth soften with their milky texture the verticality of the very high windows, lined up in enfilade, while the wall on the back is a huge mirror. Not far away, in front of the cork-lined niche at the heart of the long white bookshelves, Monsieur Saint Laurent's desk catches the eye: a plain rectangular board lined with greige baize under a sheet of glass, two wooden trestles, and that is it. The effect would be almost monastic were it not

1. Jean Cocteau, "Preface" in Alexander Liberman, *Les Maîtres de l'art contemporain* (Grenoble: Arthaud, 1961).
2. Ibid.

for the echoing accumulation of souvenirs and objects on this worktable and the photos and drawings pinned, edge to edge, on the cork of the alcove. A whole "progeny of the conscious and the unconscious"[1] that seems to emanate miraculously from a painting in which, with a few powerful lines, Bernard Buffet has captured the gentleness, the invincibility and the Proustian nostalgia of Yves Mathieu-Saint-Laurent, the sad child who had just mapped out his destiny and shaped his glory with the triumph of his *Trapèze* collection for Christian Dior. The couturier's work coat, left like a white mark on the blond back of a Scandinavian-style chair in black imitation leather, seems to extend the portrait.

A presence surrounds us, the famous "Yves' Spirit" that the Americans admired early on. Here, it is orchestrated, staged in an installation that Yves could easily have signed off with his customary "Love". White ghosts, Schläppi mannequins like Saint Laurent icons are "beautiful as a dream of stone" that has forever closed "my eyes, my wide eyes, clear as air, clear as time".[2] Like the cordons affording protection from untimely curiosity, are they there to remind us that the Oeuvre is complete and the museum nearby?

1. Ibid.
2. Charles Baudelaire, "La Beauté", *Les Fleurs du mal*, 1857.

But in this place of sublimation of memory, some of the echoes are too loud not to go straight to the heart. And now we are over-whelmed and will never be released by the vehement eloquence of these walls and these things that on countless occasions accompa-nied in an almost maternal way Yves Saint Laurent in the tortures and pleasures of what was, for him, the tragedy of creation. In a cross-fade that overleaps the constraints of the museum, the place is alive with the spirit of Yves Saint Laurent, ready to offer each woman beauty in "the wonderful silence of clothing".[1] "Saint Laurent, design for us!"[2]

He once wrote, in a movingly introspective moment: "I love above all else the rigour, the simplicity and the beauty of the classical.
"But my imagination, my pronounced gifts for invention, sometimes lead me towards the baroque, towards strangeness. That is also what keeps me from sterility, from becom-ing closed in. It's the secret of my youth, this absolute eclecticism that governs my life.
"It is said that artists see the world with the eyes of a child. I think that, in spite of all the wisdom that is the Goal of my life, I shall

1. A phrase coined by Yves Saint Laurent.
2. Freely inspired by the title of an article by Claude Berthod, "Saint Laurent coupez pour nous!" *Elle*, 7 March 1968.

continue to see life with the eyes of a child, my life, but most of all my work."[1]

These few words say it all.

This confession, which is infinitely touching in its lucid sincerity, is perhaps the pass key to the inner world, to all the schizophrenic conflicts of an extraordinary artistic experience that is fascinating in its intensity. By the illuminating light of this psychoanalysis, we have a better idea of how, "by travelling through his personal shadows",[2] the couturier managed to construct his identity and, finally, conquer freedom, by building a style: his own. The Saint Laurent style.

In the beginning, for the sensitive, pensive little boy who liked to play at dressing his puppets there was just the animal pleasure of the sea and Oran, "all sun and inky shadows",[3] and the reassurance of surrounding female presences: a grandmother, a great-aunt, younger sisters and, above all, a mother whose "sapphire-blue" eyes fascinated him.[4] An adored mother, a socialite, frivolous and very elegant, with a passion

1. Text written by Yves Saint Laurent on headed notepaper from 55 Rue de Babylone Paris 7.

2. Jean Cocteau, "Preface" in Alexander Liberman, *op. cit.*

3. Anthony Burgess, "All About Yves", *The New York Times Magazine*, 11 September 1977.

4. Handwritten text by Yves Saint Laurent preparing for an interview with Laurence Benaïm for an article in *Marie Claire* (November 1995) on the subject of "Couturiers and Their Mothers".

for beautiful dresses. She was his first vision of fashion in that cosmopolitan, glittering world of Oran, with its endless round of parties. As he would later reveal, "With my mother I experienced rare moments of happiness. This is private. My sensitivity about her is extreme. To talk about her is like extracting from my heart a substance that hurts me."[1]

Then came the shock of school, years of torture that would leave him traumatized for life. Now, for the first time, he experienced the pain of exclusion, the pitiless cruelty of his fellow pupils. They rejected him as "the poet" – the supreme insult. A timid, pensive poet astray in their world. The playground was synonymous with mortification, the chapel a precarious shelter. That left the refuge of a kind of schizophrenia.

On one side, he was the school whipping boy, incapable of talking about his torments, even if he swore to himself that he would have his revenge, that he would see "my name up in lights on the Champs-Élysées".[2] On the other, the gaiety of the family home with the everyday escape of the little cardboard theatre

1. Ibid.
2. Preparatory text by Yves Saint Laurent for the exhibition catalogue "Yves Saint Laurent" at the Costume Institute of the Metropolitan Museum, 22 July 1983.

that he had built for himself, making all the sets and costumes and even the paper figures that performed the plays of which he was the author. He was at ease with "fictions and unrealities",[1] and practised, "day after day what, a few years later, would become the techniques of his métier. From birth, he was destined for the game of embellishing and transforming."[2]

Sometimes, he would get lost, delighted to find himself in the exquisite labyrinth of "La Recherche", imagining himself to be a kind of Monsieur Swann. The impeccable khaki desert shirts worn by the American soldiers who landed in Algeria also made an impression, as did the "navy blue, and the white uniforms of the navy officers", and all the glamour on display in the harbour, because "they were close to death".[3]

And he drew, still, and always more, manically. Magazine figures, mainly, inspired by the line of Christian Bérard, that "impeccable servant of beauty",[4] whom he admired equally for his fashion drawings and theatre sets. Theatre and fashion would be the two

1. Waldemar-George, "Christian Bérard", *Formes*, no. 1, December 1929–January 1930.
2. Edmonde Charles-Roux, "Yves Saint Laurent, ce petit lycéen qui nous vient d'Oran", *Le Figaro littéraire*, 12 February 1968.
3. "Yves Saint Laurent: The Genius of Style", interview with Joan Juliet Buck, *Vogue US*, December 1983.
4. Jean Cocteau, "Hommage à Christian Bérard", *Vogue Paris*, March 1949.

poles between which the little schoolboy from Oran stretched his talents, uncertain which to choose. Until destiny decided for him.

Yves always dreamed of Paris as a magical place where he would at last be able to concentrate on all the things he really enjoyed. Having passed his baccalaureate, he set off to meet Michel de Brunhoff, director of *Vogue*, who was also a friend of his parents, taking a letter of introduction. He also took a handful of drawings that were deemed "very amusing".[1] "The little Saint Laurent got here yesterday," wrote Michel de Brunhoff to his editor Edmonde Charles-Roux. "To my amazement, at least twenty of the fifty drawings he brought me could have been by Dior. I have never met anyone more gifted in my whole life. I asked at once that he be given an interview, telling Dior that if I was so insistent it was to prove to him that there could be no question of leaks, since our child had come off the boat the day before and Christian's collection was only two days old. I shall be bringing him along, holding his hand, later … Just be there! … If this small boy turns out to be great one day, you will remember me."[2]

1. André Parinaud, "Yves Mathieu-Saint-Laurent," *Arts*, 9–15 April 1958.
2. Edmonde Charles-Roux, *op. cit.*

On 20 June 1955, Yves Mathieu-Saint-Laurent joined the Maison Dior. He was not yet nineteen, and would never forget his debt to this happy coincidence: "For me, working for Christian Dior was a miracle. I admired him inordinately. He was the most famous couturier of the day, but he had also succeeded in creating a unique couture house and surrounding himself with people who were irreplaceable. ... He taught me the roots of my art. I owe him a large part of my life and, whatever may have happened since, I have never forgotten the years spent at his side."[1]

The master's sudden and unexpected death thrust his admiring pupil into the spotlight: for he was the dauphin, Monsieur Dior's anointed successor at the head of his empire: aged only twenty-one, here he was directing the biggest couture house in the world. In a state of complete euphoria, almost playfully, he prepared and presented his first collection, and it was only after the footlights illuminating the global triumph of his perfect young ladies in *Trapèze* dresses had gone out, that the anxiety insidiously took hold, never to let go: "Like the trapeze artist who for the first time, sizes up the yawning

1. Preparatory text by Yves Saint Laurent for the exhibition catalogue "Yves Saint Laurent", *op. cit.*

emptiness under the astral brightness of the spotlights",[1] he would now and always be "that amused child playing dice on the edge of the abyss".[2]

Highly strung children are often fragile. The ordeal of military service would shatter the élan of this young man who, in only six collections, had become "the Little Prince of couture". Laid low by depression, he spent two and a half hellish months in the Val de Grâce military hospital, between electric shocks, sadistic inmates and chemical straitjackets. Yves was terrified, ground down, deeply and enduringly scarred, wounded and traumatized. The seismic psychic violence inflicted at Val de Grâce deeply affected his exacerbated sensitivity, just like the secret persecutions of his schooldays in Oran. But, like Proust, his favourite writer, he was proud to belong to "that splendid and pitiable family" of the supersensitive, "which is the salt of the earth. ... It is they and they alone who found religions and create great works."[3]

1. Edmonde Charles-Roux, *op. cit.*
2. Jean-Jacques Schuhl, *Libération*, 7 January 2002.
3. From the third volume of *Remembrance of Things Past* (*À la recherche du temps perdu*), published in its original French as *Le côté de Guermantes* in 1921–22. Marcel Proust, *The Guermantes Way*, trans. C. K. Scott Moncrieff and Terence Kilmartin (Vintage, 1982), 315.

"There was something of the exterminating angel"[1] in this young man, and it was Pierre Bergé, who had "everything [that] he didn't have",[2] who would coax him into a redemptive reaction.

Their paths had crossed after the prodigy's first collection at Dior. Now Pierre would be there for Yves, every day. "I remember telling you on your hospital bed ... that you were no longer at the head of the couture house that employed you ...: 'Well,' you said, 'you and I will found one, and you will run it'."[3] They had no money, and the Saint Laurent name had disappeared from the haute couture salons. They were taking a risk, a mad risk, but Bergé's faith in the young couturier was unshakeable. And as they edged their way from one makeshift solution to the next, from the tiny two rooms in Rue La Boétie rented with their savings, to the attic workshops of Rue Jean-Goujon, a dusty left-over from the Maison Manguin, the wager gradually became less mad.

While, between two bouts of despondency, Yves produced more than three thousand

1. Edmonde Charles-Roux, *op. cit.*

2. Interview with Yves Saint Laurent in David Teboul's film, *Le Temps retrouvé*, 2001.

3. Pierre Bergé, *Lettres à Yves* (Paris: Gallimard, 2010).

sketches, Pierre worked tirelessly, selling a few paintings, an apartment. Parlaying his reputation as a genius of publicity,[1] he even tried a few "media coups". And, miraculously, after all this time in the wilderness, a patron appeared. Who was it? No one knew. "Apparently, it's a secret."[2] The rumour mill was grinding away among the effervescent socialites of Paris.

In a feverish rush, the workshops were moved to 30 bis Rue Spontini, once the townhouse of the painter Jean-Louis Forain, It was repaired, the roof raised, the interiors repainted. Like veiled phantoms, the models were transported at night, shrouded in mystery, from the provisional workshops in Rue Jean-Goujon. Paris was alive with a thousand murmurs and the world of fashion was burning with impatience to witness what looked set to be a historical morning.[3]

On 29 January 1962, the presentation of the first collection signed by Yves Saint Laurent was "drowned in applause". "Saint Laurent's 'solo' closed the fashion parade," proclaimed

1. Dino Buzzati, "Le 'Solo' de Saint Laurent a clos la parade de la mode", *Corriere della Sera*, 30 January 1962.
2. Sylvain Zegel, "La crise de la couture n'aura pas lieu", *Arts*, 24–30 January 1962.
3. The Maison Yves Saint Laurent stayed in Rue Spontini until 14 July 1974, the official date of its move to 5 Avenue Marceau, its definitive address.

Dino Buzzati's headline in the *Corriere della Sera*. "The pale young man made an appearance but was seen for only a short moment, for soon he was surrounded by female admirers, hugging him and kissing him." Yves Mathieu-Saint-Laurent had taken "the great exam, with only his personal strength to call on", and the "frail and timid prince of haute couture", "the loveable gazelle with glasses", the dauphin of Christian Dior, had "become independent" by "creating his own house". Now the house of "YSL" needed to truly exist.

It was the exceptional, almost metaphysical pact between the couturier and Pierre Bergé that would make this existence historic. In this unique alliance between an "inspired reed"[1] and a man with a talent for managing business as if writing a bestseller with Yves as its hero, each kept strictly to his assigned role: Yves the creator, Pierre the strategist. "I prepared the ammunition, the provisions and the troops, you fought the battle … [and] led us from one victory to another."[2] Bergé understood that for the dazzling miracle of creativity to occur time and time and time again, Saint Laurent needed to live within a

1. Edmonde Charles-Roux, interviewed by Laurence Benaïm, *Le Monde*, supplement, 23 January 2002.
2. Pierre Bergé, *op. cit.*

bubble of illusion, free of the constraints of real life, protected from everything. A closed world, a cinematic trompe l'oeil dedicated to beauty where, facing the "great mirrors"[1] of his studio, the couturier could dwell intimately with his "aesthetic ghosts". Without them, he said, "I could not live".[2]

Monsieur Saint Laurent's studio on Avenue Marceau was nothing like the old-fashioned "office of dreams" cherished by Christian Dior. It was a potent place, half hell and half paradise, shaped by all the anguished yet formative paradoxes that made Saint Laurent so endlessly fascinating. Anxieties, joys and fervour. Yves Saint Laurent had his superstitious side. Forming a surprising installation halfway between "rigour and profusion",[3] a thousand objects were amassed in his studio, some of them strange. These ex-votos and gris-gris had the value of the memories they stood for. Monsieur Dior's magic cane, a whole dynasty of porcelain miniatures of Moujik, his adored little bulldog, portraits

1. Speech by Yves Saint Laurent, Saint Catherine, 24 November 1989 – Trans. Saint Catherine of Alexandria was the patron saint of milliners and couture.
2. Letter of thanks from Yves Saint Laurent to Hervé Guibert for an article published in *Le Monde* on 8 December 1983.
3. Hector Bianciotti, "La rigueur et le foisonnant", *Le Monde*, supplement, 23 January 2002.

of beloved and admired individuals, a few trophies from his career, a ten of clubs chanced upon in the cellars at Rue Spontini, and the tiny silver hand he used as a paperweight and lucky charm – there would be no end to this inventory whose Saint-Laurentian logic relates the sensitive archaeology of a "heart still divided between constancy and change".[1]

The studio of Yves Saint Laurent is a sanctuary. It is the sacred place where his "glorifications of woman"[2] were ceremonially accomplished, the home of his "idols", where he performed all the secret rites of the artist/artisan calling that was his one and only raison d'être. At once refuge and prison, "ossuary and womb",[3] it was that unique place where all the couturier's creative powers converged.

There, "between dagger and poison",[4] was the beating heart of Saint Laurent's Oeuvre.

It all began with anguish. An irrepressible anguish. First of all, there was the extreme

1. Preparatory text by Yves Saint Laurent for the exhibition catalogue "Yves Saint Laurent", *op. cit.*

2. Anthony Burgess, *op. cit.*

3. Yves Saint Laurent quoted by Mariella Righini, "Saint Laurent : vingt sur vingt", *Le Nouvel Observateur*, 30 January 1982.

4. Pierre Bergé, *op. cit.*

violence of a profession that he adored, yet which, implacably, four times a year, demanded the paralysing descent into hell where everything must be called into question. There was the brutal aggression of the factitious novelty demanded by the press, waiting like a wild beast for its prey; and the unbearable cruelty of perfidious rumour, of the ferociously judging eye, the peremptory words that destroyed without seeing or understanding. And then, that suffocating terror of the void, the obsession and despair of the confrontation with the "inaccessible star", that half-glimpsed "nothing" that is "everything".[1] A blind immersion in darkness, yet with the instinctive knowledge that at the end of the night there would always be that burst of radiant light.

To survive the paralysing, crucifying torture of anxiety, the only solution for Saint Laurent was Marrakech and the oasis of serenity he created with Pierre Bergé. Perhaps, for this son of the Mediterranean, this Proustian nostalgic for all the skies of Oran, and for the tender, joyous heavens of early childhood, it may have offered a sort of kindly analytic cure that on each occasion allowed him to murder the past while keeping faith with his

1. Allusion to one of Yves Saint Laurent's favourite phrases: "It is everything and it is nothing".

origins. The sun of Morocco seemed to him even more beautiful than the sun of Algeria. He soaked in the soothing luxuriance of trees and flowers. "In Marrakech, I rest my mind clear. I feel good. ... On every street corner ... one sees groups that are impressive in their intensity, their relief ... evoking Delacroix's sketches ... [and which] are in fact simply the improvisation of life."[1] Solitude, indolence, sensuality, contemplation in the pursuit of a certain truth. Only the *Opium* of Marrakech could lead him to the limits of the world, of his world.

And then there was this intense happiness of a child marvelling at the knowledge that he had at last "discovered the precious message".[2] "How many times did I imagine myself powerless, fragile, desperate before the blackness of habit, and how many times was the curtain torn, offering me a glimpse of the unlimited horizons that have given me the greatest joys and, allow me to say this, real pride."[3] His inhibitions swept away, Saint Laurent would now get to work at dizzying speed, never letting up until the collection

1. "Portrait de l'artiste", interview by Yvonne Baby, *Le Monde*, 8 December 1983.
2. Text written by Yves Saint Laurent on headed notepaper from 55 Rue de Babylone Paris 7.
3. Preparatory text by Yves Saint Laurent for the exhibition catalogue "Yves Saint Laurent", *op. cit.*

was complete. Even doubt, if it arose, could be resolved by this dizziness. He drew, without pause, very fast, without thinking, as if in a state of grace. Extra-lucid. He called this the unpredictable "miracle of the moment". "The line."[1]

On ream after ream of white paper, sketch followed sketch, like the magic flow of the imagination in automatic-writing mode. "When I pick up a pencil, I don't know what I am going to draw. … I start with a woman's face and suddenly the dress follows, the clothing resolves itself. … It is creation in its pure state, without preparations, without vision. … When the drawing is finished, I am very happy."[2]

Twice a year, in early June and early December, Yves Saint Laurent would thus fly out to Marrakech for a fortnight and return with a little case in rust-red leather, monstrously stuffed with sketches. As the obligatory prelude, the ritual of this quest for the Grail in Morocco is where both the myth and the history of each Saint Laurent haute couture collection was first written.

On the Avenue Marceau, time stood still in the wait for the revelation of these precious

1. Interview with Yves Saint Laurent in David Teboul's film, *op. cit.*
2. Ibid.

and prodigiously eloquent sketches. "He put out so many ideas!" recalls his faithful second, Anne-Marie Muñoz. "There was everything, and it all came out just like that."[1] And, from the *cabine des mannequins* – "those demoiselles of the salon" as Helmut Newton called them – to the workshops on the second floor, everyone knew now that Monsieur Saint Laurent had "found it" and everyone felt ready to follow him, in a state of total admiration and absolute trust, all the way. "Everything at this point is wonderful," wrote Saint Laurent. "For three weeks, with my workshop, my studio, I and the whole house live through a wonderful and exciting adventure."[2] "I am surrounded by a tremendous team that I adore and which feels the same way about me."[3] The couture house, with Pierre Bergé at its helm, was like a vast conspiracy where everyone was determined to "spare" him. The password? "LOVE." Between effervescence and silence, feverish activity and fraught meditation, wild laughter and mischievous gaiety, the studio now became the magic stage, the intimate theatre of a five-act play that might be titled

1. Rushes of the interview with Anne-Marie Muñoz by David Teboul, 2001.
2. Text written by Yves Saint Laurent on headed notepaper from 55 Rue de Babylone Paris 7.
3. Jean-Dominique Bauby and Francine Vormèse, "Saint Laurent : 30 ans de passion", *Elle*, 27 January 1992.

"Couture and Sentiments." Its tall door was usually ajar, open to the noises of the House. Under the authority of the studio director, Anne-Marie Muñoz, and the poetic, energizing gaze of Loulou de La Falaise, the *premières* and *premiers d'atelier* (workroom heads), *mannequins cabine*, embroiderers and favoured suppliers joined and succeeded one another in keeping with a protocol faithfully inspired by the House of Dior. Still, if Saint Laurent's need for calm and solitude became too imperious, he would close that door, posting words from Silvana Mangano written in his own hand: *Comportatevi bene*. Now only the density of the silence in the holy of holies manifested the couturier's presence. Unless, that is, a few curious workers dared to indulge in the secret rite of the dormer window. In fact, few could resist the temptation. An oeil-de-boeuf window on the workshop floor afforded a view straight into the studio, revealing the figure of the couturier "bent over the table where he drew and wrote, half-child and half-monument, so distant and so present".[1]

The first act could be titled "The Revelation of the Drawings".

1. Laurence Benaïm, "Les préparatifs de la dernière collection", *Le Monde*, supplement, 23 January 2002.

Since the return from Marrakech, they have been jealously hidden away in the studio chest. It falls to Anne-Marie Muñoz to summon the *premiers d'atelier* to this key rite. Emotions run high, impatience vying with curiosity, but all are certain that the paths along which they are about to be led are sure, that the new collection is already much more than a promise.

Doffing his white coat, as if to mark the importance of this ceremony of discovery, Monsieur Saint Laurent greets them surrounded by a mass of sketches in black and white, spread over tables, or in front of the great mirror, on the carpet. Here Marguerite Duras's words about Saint Laurent come to mind: "Like a writer, every day he writes as if it were the first time, I could swear it ... He does what we were waiting for, every year. I mean that he does what we did not know we were waiting for."[1] "Noise and Silence." Boundless admiration for the abstraction embodied by his incisive line. Some may venture a remark about this or that expressive detail of a sketch. All are mesmerized, stunned. Still, choices now have to be made. The very private, one-on-one meetings with

1. Preface by Marguerite Duras, "Le Bruit et le Silence" in *Yves Saint Laurent et la photographie de mode* (Paris: Albin Michel, 1988).

the workshop heads – *Flou* (dresses and gowns) and *Tailleur* (jackets and skirts) – will be decisive.

The precise moment of this second act – "The Attribution of the Drawings" – may come immediately or be slightly delayed, but not too long: there are barely three weeks to go before the collection will be airborne. Wearing his white coat this time, the couturier waits, sitting at a worktable covered with dossiers of sketches, carefully organized into categories following the etiquette of haute couture: tailleurs (suits), evening dresses, day dresses, cocktail dresses, blouses, furs, etc. Usually, this sequence is initiated by the oldest member of the *Tailleur* workshop. Throughout the studio you can sense a potent emotion, a kind of microclimate where, in an alchemy of modesty and love, the couturier's timidity melds with the certitudes of the visionary, and his expectancy, waiting to see how the collection will grow when the sketches are interpreted by all those with an intimate, inside knowledge of the Saint Laurent rhetoric. Now, looking at the drawings spread over a table, they can ask questions. "We knew that he was really expecting something from us, and gave us great freedom." It is a respectful dialogue.

Change a waistline. Soften a shoulder. Raising a collar. "You must choose what you prefer, Jean-Pierre." And so, choices are made. And if, in this orgy of drawn ideas, a look the couturier particularly liked seems to have been forgotten, he will gently insist, "Oh look, Jean-Pierre! Don't you like that one?"[1] And, before going back up to his studio, Jean-Pierre adds the precious ensemble to the forty drawings already selected.

Next comes the crucial phase of making the first sketch of the model, in couture cloth for *Tailleur* items and butter muslin (cheesecloth) for the *Flou*. The cloth must capture the drawing exactly, and add life. This, as they used to say at Dior, is work for "partners". From the *secondes* to the "little bees", the whole workshop takes part, but it is the privilege of the *premier d'atelier* to translate into three dimensions the demanding precision of Saint Laurent's line. The visual interpretation of the drawing is thus vital to "setting it up" in such a way as to truly express the soul of the design. To an expert eye, the clarity of a Saint Laurent sketch says everything, in a few pencil lines: the nature and direction of the fabric, bias or with the

1. Interview with Jean-Pierre Derbord, former premier of the *Tailleur* atelier and technical director of workshops at the Maison Yves Saint Laurent, Paris, January 2014.

grain, the movement, the hang, the sleeve properly squared, not too little and not too much, and even what cannot be put into words, simply from the way a hand rests on the hips. "It is a story without words."[1] The rest is all a matter of métier.

Then comes "The Day of the Toiles" a more theatrical third act, "moving, decisive and hard, too, for that is when I try to discover the secret of the collection," wrote Saint Laurent.[2] Its choreography is highly ritualized. Sketch in hand, each *premier* takes his or her turn to come down to the studio accompanied by the chosen *mannequin cabine* to "pose", "play the cloth". From his architect's table, Monsieur Saint Laurent watches for her entrance in the mirror, and it is a success if he recognizes his drawing. If he cannot acknowledge his paternity, the model is rejected, albeit with endless amounts of respect and kindness. "Monsieur Saint Laurent does not like to upset his *premières* who do not like to displease him."[3] "Each collection has its secret. I try to find a way of recapturing the spirit of the cloth, of keeping in fabric the naivety of a toile, its

1. Ibid.
2. Text by Yves Saint Laurent, Paris, May 1990.
3. Interview with Violeta Sanchez, former *mannequin cabine* at the Maison Yves Saint Laurent, Paris, April 2014.

beauty, its magical character. So, a bit of time goes by. The fabrics arrive and everything falls into place."[1]

This fourth act, when "The Fabrics Make Their Entrance", so that each toile may find the one that's right for it, is the passionate and joyous intermezzo of this drama that is the birth a Saint Laurent collection. It is a unique moment of delectation, of religious sensuality, which can also be meditative and grave, when these fabrics which take over the studio are attributed. Crêpes, chiffons, precious silks, grains de poudre – Saint Laurent's black gold – and all the wonderful, exclusive prints from Abraham, specially designed for the couturier by Gustav Zumsteg: "Gustav Zumsteg, my ally, my friend and my partner. I made my finest dresses in his fabrics. His talent was often an endless source of inspiration."[2]

Fabric gets everywhere. Rolls stand like colourful totems against the tables and in the window bays, swatches hang over chair backs, the bookshelves are a rainbow-coloured cornucopia of samples and the carpet a patchwork of widths of material and hangers feverishly thrown down for

1. Text by Yves Saint Laurent, Paris, May 1990.
2. Text by Yves Saint Laurent in homage to forty-five years of collaboration with Gustav Zumsteg, June 2005.

inspection. The Fabric God is in his heaven, and his bespectacled high priest is leading the worship, dressed in his white-coat vestment, given a muted echo by the toile that the mannequin "poses" like a dress. A handful of acolytes attend and, naturally, the two vestals, "she who knows, watches over and observes", Anne-Marie Muñoz, and Loulou, the "lightness of crystal",[1] with her catalysing instinct. Unrolling and feeling the heft of a crêpe, wondering about a black, assessing the hand, the feel of a grain de poudre, the swish of seductive chiffons. Yves Saint Laurent is the magisterial high priest of this necessary rite of creating "effects", and his cane is always near. He searches, handles the fabric until he knows what the results will be. Eyes trained on the mirror, he lets a sample of silk flow from the shoulders to the feet, sculpts the sketch of a dress directly on the model's body, and eventually finds or recaptures its natural form. The eye examines, the silence speaks, the silence explodes. "The toile carries in it the Magic of the drawing. One must be very attentive to the toile before choosing the fabric in which it will be made in order to recapture the Magic

1. Speech by Yves Saint Laurent at the traditional lunch following the spring-summer 1983 haute couture show on 26 January 1983.

of the sketch."[1] And Monsieur Saint Laurent decides.

When a fabric has finally been found that seems most likely to meet and not betray the imperative expectations of the toile, a sample is cut, pinned on, and everything goes back to the workshop, with the drawing, for the final phase.

To perform, in the allotted time, this fifth act, that of the "Secret Births of the Designs", the *Flou*, the *Tailleur*, and all the workshops, drunk on the knowledge that they are "the architects and masons of Monsieur Saint Laurent's taste",[2] start working with their fabrics in order to initiate the metamorphosis of the toiles into clothing: to create the miracle. Working with chalk, tape measure, needle and pins, snipping with squeaking scissors, they must find the proportions, volumes and energy of the fabric. Here the millimetre is the unit of measurement and the couturier's sketch the absolute template. The process is a dogged pursuit of perfection in an almost mute effervescence. Here, everything whispers and works in a confident and hushed

1. Handwritten text by Yves Saint Laurent.
2. Madame Arlette, *première d'atelier Flou*, quoted by Laetitia d'Ornano, "Histoire d'une robe haute couture", *Madame Figaro*, 14 February 1998.

solidarity, beyond words. The murmuring silence of the workshops is almost like that of "long-united lovers who no longer need to explain themselves to understand each other".[1]

As soon as a dress is judged sufficiently developed to be put before the Grand Jury, *premières* and *secondes*, full of pride and anxious doubts, escort their *mannequin* to the holy of holies for a first, tense judgement. "Will he recognize his drawing?" Thus begin hours and days of toing and froing between workshops and studio, a long processional ballet of fittings, each one a drama of love and anxiety. The rigour is infinite, the eye of Monsieur Saint Laurent as pitiless as it is tender when it comes to judging the fit between the dress and his dream. "I expect everything of my workshops, of their exquisite and immaculate work. That is what couture is all about!"[2]

In the great mirror of the studio, Amalia, a cardinal character in our play, moves hieratically forward in a narrow black skirt and a blouse in white organdie. Monsieur Saint Laurent watches. Silence. And the model, who does not yet know what this silence means,

1. Philippe Utz, "*Love*", *Numéro*, February 2002.
2. Simone Baron, "La naissance secrète du modèle n° 1043", *Le Journal du dimanche*, 28 January 1979.

moves impassibly on her high heels, with the lofty grace of a goddess. In the language of the Maison, "She has the star".

The *première* and the two guardian angels, Anne-Marie and Loulou, are also studying the mirror, holding their breath. Now the oracle speaks: "It's beautiful, all this white! It's a divine blouse! But the skirt ... a bit tighter at the bottom, I think." "More restricted?" "Yes, that's it ... I can see it now." He smiles reassuringly and the *première* stands. "Now we're going to finish and fine-tune a bit. ... It'll be right tomorrow."

Other times – most usually – the ecstasy is immediate, and recognition likewise. "It's a dream! Esther, what a pretty dress that is! So light! 'Thank you, sir.' You aren't too tired? 'It's all right, sir, we'll manage.'"

"That is ravishing, my dear Georgette!"

On one occasion, by grace or by magic, by daring to add honey-coloured *envol* at the bottom of the ebony sheath that had been asked for, the inspired talent of a *première* revealed, at the fitting, an unexpected truth of model no. 87 in the spring-summer 2001 haute couture collection: "Colette! I asked you for a 'sausage'[1] and you have made me a masterpiece! It's sensational! It's quite marvellous,

1. Couture jargon for a sheath dress.

my dear Colette! That skirt! That ruffle ... Extraordinary!"[1] Monsieur Saint Laurent takes his *première* in his arms. The emotion spreads and everyone applauds.

"I do not think," said Saint Laurent in one of his Saint Catherine's day speeches, "I do not think that we are ever more fascinated, dazzled, astonished than when we are working in front of the big mirrors of the studio on a model and everything is transformed, takes flight in another way, ending in gaiety, admiration of this perfection. ... We do not say it, but you have won. And you forget how hard you have had to work in your workshops."[2]

"My children, ... my talents beyond talent, my tendernesses, my queens, my kings and my princesses,"[3] he also said to these men and women he loved like a family, and as the best workshop in the world.

And, for Yves Saint Laurent, after the headiness of triumph on the podium and the ovation that greeted no. 87, statuesquely set off

1. Dialogue between Yves Saint Laurent and his *première*, Colette in David Teboul's film, *Yves Saint Laurent 5 avenue Marceau 75116 Paris*, 2001.

2. Speech by Yves Saint Laurent, Saint Catherine, 24 November 1989.

3. Speech by Yves Saint Laurent at the traditional lunch after the autumn-winter 1988–1989 haute couture show, Paris, Hôtel de Crillon, 27 July 1988.

by supermodel Alek Wek, the drama came to an end, with a heart-rending smile over that infinitely cruel emptiness that leaves you feeling like an orphan when it's all over. *Post coitum anima tristis est* said the Ancients.[1]

So many fears, sleepless nights and dazzling triumphs disappearing into "the cold night of oblivion"![2] All these ideas that shot forth like meteorites, fatally doomed to "disappear like the ones before, like those to follow"[3] when one was dreaming of eternal creation: "What a thing it is, for those who really desired only that!"[4]

Might not the bitter taste of that frustration have also helped orient Saint Laurent towards the ardent, instinctive quest for his style? That conquest of "the place and the formula", as Arthur Rimbaud would have said,[5] is probably one of the most intimate truths of the studio.

"An unrepentant homosexual, you loved women, you said so loud and clear," wrote Pierre Bergé in his *Lettres à Yves*. An illumination, an obsessive idolatry since his childhood in Oran, which came to channel all the artistic

1. "After love, the soul is sad."
2. Jacques Prévert, *Les Feuilles mortes*, 1946.
3. Françoise Sagan, "Saint Laurent par Françoise Sagan", quotation by Yves Saint Laurent, *Elle*, 3 March 1980.
4. Anna de Noailles, *L'Ombre des jours*, 1902.
5. Arthur Rimbaud, "Vagabonds", *Illuminations*, 1872–75.

gifts of this super-gifted creator, besieged by his own ideas, a man who could have achieved his dreams of beauty as much by the magic of words or the spells of theatre sets as by inventing the lover's discourse of dresses. By a fascinating paradox, the mysterious reality of a woman's body is the secret code affording access to Saint Laurent's truest self. From that reality, in barely ten years, Saint Laurent constructed his own identity by constructing his style. The progress is powerful, stunning.

Starting from the already outmoded school of his master, Christian Dior, he succeeded in keeping what was best about it: the profundity, the seriousness of the professionalism. But, in the logic of the abyss of his contradictory neuroses, this fervent Proustian was already a superstar of Warholian immediacy. From the outset, he sensed the unconfessed desire of women still stifled by the reminiscences of an outmoded New Look, their wish to live in clothing that appropriated its times, free as a sigh and, like them, seductive.

Starting with his first collections for Dior, this "sadistic or advanced child"[1] jettisoned paddings and whalebones, banishing the

1. A reference to the subtitle of *La Vilaine Lulu*, a comic Yves Saint Laurent created at Dior, *Contes pour enfants sadiques ou avancés* (Paris: Tchou, 1967).

house's iconic "line". "The main element of this fashion is youth and, above all, simplicity, naturalness, suppleness … There is not really much of a line in my collection. That indeed is one of the main points. Up to now, fashion was framed in a purely geometrical form with a more constructed design. This time there is relaxation, a suppleness. Yes, I think that line is going, in favour of a style."[1] This was an almost unconscious and very decorous way of telling the television reporter who was interviewing him, beneath the portrait of Christian Dior, both that he had changed fashion and that he *was* fashion, a bit like Flaubert exclaiming, "Madame Bovary c'est moi!" Whether in a premonition, or by simple journalistic formula, *L'Express* even described several skirt suits with straight jackets as a "personal version of the Chanel tailleur". And a few months was all Saint Laurent needed to get away from Diorised woman, not only by evoking the Chanel look in its freedom, but also by daring to leave the salons for the street so as to give women the means of power, while finding the power of his own style.

1. Christian Dior spring-summer 1959 collection.

Style ... The word was deliberate and there would be no going back. *Rebelle* ... *Avant-Garde* ... *Quatre Cents Coups* ... *Zazie* ... and the names of other models in the last collection he showed at Dior signposted the path ahead.[1] The "scandalous" *Chicago* blouson in black patent leather with crocodile embossing and edging in mink showed that Yves Saint Laurent had truly broken free.

Henceforth, his nostalgias would be rebellious ones. Which is why, now and again, his aesthetic, placed by inclination under the auspices of a resolutely modern hyper-classicism, succumbed in a state of ecstasy to the unexpected flamboyance of exotic sagas, or gave in to the very adolescent desire to do "exactly what he wanted" – exactly, and immediately, as with his so-called "scandalous" collection of summer 1971 – his "favourite"[2]: "I prefer to shock rather than to bore by repeating."[3]

In the summer of 1965, three years after the opening of the Maison Saint Laurent in Rue Spontini, the "Mondrian" collection

1. Christian Dior autumn-winter 1960 collection.
2. "Casser le bon goût", interview by Mariella Righini, *Le Nouvel Observateur*, 16 August 1971.
3. Claude Berthod, "La libération de la femme selon Saint Laurent", *Elle*, 1 March 1971.

pulverized the stiffness of traditional elegance with its "mobile" dresses. Haute couture they certainly were, but he could already picture them seducing the streets of Saint-Germain-des-Prés.[1]

The *rive gauche*[2] revolution, "an operation to reach out to youth never before tried by a great couturier", was his own deliberate doing, for he "wanted to see his dresses come out onto the street". This was the catalyst and guiding thread that led him to the apotheosis of his style, that is to say, "clothes that are 'suitable', serious and responsible"[3] and yet – and this is the mystery of Saint Laurent – different, like "a fixed reverie that would change from year to year".[4] A universal wardrobe that, in its irresistible, androgynous composition, would overturn all the barriers of sex, age and season decreed by fashion. The pea coat, no. 82, which opened the inaugural show of 1962, was a precursor. The Saint Laurent tuxedo, that radical uniform in all its variations, that "ghost of future nocturnal luxury",[5] which incited the wearer to mobilize her

1. Reference to Yves Saint Laurent's interview in *Women's Wear Daily*, 11 October 1965.
2. SAINT LAURENT *rive gauche*: name of the ready-to-wear line launched in September 1966.
3. Claude Berthod, *op. cit.*
4. Marcel Proust, *Le côté de Guermantes*, 1921–22, *op. cit.*
5. Arthur Rimbaud, "Vagabonds", *op. cit.*

femininity to an extreme degree, while under-scoring with its black the power that she had conquered, had become the eternal YSL icon. In 1983, after the first Yves Saint Laurent retrospective at the Metropolitan Museum in New York, the ruminating couturier told Yvonne Baby and *Le Monde*: "In 1960, one could say that I had my felicities, but you could not have spoken of style." In 1972, the style was most definitely there. Having found and established it, he would never cease to "affirm, refine and renew it".[1] As Pierre Bergé admiringly noted, "Yves Saint Laurent died in 2008. He could have died in 1972, the oeuvre was already there. There was no waste. All Saint Laurent was created in ten years."[2] And for those who can read them, who can hear the music of the walls that witnessed this history, his studio soon appears as the signal place of the "magic study" and poetic adven-ture "that founded what remains".[3]

"A place of life, an artist's studio", it really is the place where he was able to conceive and "develop something that had not been done before".[4]

1. "Portrait de l'artiste", interview by Yvonne Baby, *op. cit.*
2. Interview with Pierre Bergé, April 2014, Paris.
3. Inspired by Hölderlin.
4. Interview with Philippe Sollers on the occasion of the publica-tion of *Studio*, 1997: www.gallimard.fr.

What trace did he wish to leave? "That of an artist who created an oeuvre"[1] Saint Laurent once told journalists interviewing him about his thirty years of passion. "I shall never stop creating. It is my reason for living."[2] We cannot deny artist status to someone who, day after day, at the cost of such intense suffering, sacrificed everything to the construction of his work, his cathedral, and who, with a kind of folly, persisted in his quest for his "fundamental tone",[3] offering his whole life for this goal.

Although, with the rigour and intellectual honesty that were in his heart, he so often claimed to be "an artisan at the most, in a kind of artistic profession",[4] it would be a betrayal not to recognize in this eminently exact poet of this fashion that he hated, an artist "seeded with mystery".[5] Saint Laurent was viscerally creative. His quest for beauty meant the celebration of women's bodies. His drawings were beautiful, his models, blueprints for emotion. But Saint Laurent, that eternal Proustian child with visions of

1. Jean-Dominique Bauby and Francine Vormèse, *op. cit.*
2. Ibid.
3. Martin Heidegger, *Les Hymnes de Hölderlin*, trans. F. Fédier and J. Hervier (Paris: Gallimard, 1988). He talks about the "fundamental tone of poetry".
4. Preface by Bernard-Henri Lévy in *Yves Saint Laurent par Yves Saint Laurent* (Paris: Herscher, 1986).
5. Marcel Proust, *Sodome et Gomorrhe*, 1921–22.

beauty perpetually torn between the poign-
ant feeling of lost time still hanging on and
the immediate urgency of the fleeting present that he captured, like a super-clairvoy-
ant medium, thanks to "secret antennae
that enable him to know, without seeing
anything or hearing anything",[1] Saint Laurent, that *voyageur immobile*, was well aware
that between the inspired line of the sketch
and its sublime accomplishment as a dress,
there lay the absolute gaze, professional
expertise, and the immediate confrontation
with the movements of the *mannequin* and
the fabric.

At once the prison and refuge of the
self-chosen recluse, the studio was above all
the magic lair from which might flare the
mental alchemy and sorcery of Saint Laurent.
There, in his inner solitude, he could let himself go to the pleasures of projecting dreams,
and wait, with amorous anxiety, for all the
"fellow travellers"[2] who escorted him on his
escapes. Memories and wounds: *Harper's
Bazaar* and *Vogue* in the big library in Oran.
The theatre, the metaphor and the measure
of the sets by Christian Bérard. Diaghilev

1. Jean-Dominique Bauby and Francine Vormèse, *op. cit.*
2. "Inspirateurs", from a quotation by Yves Saint Laurent, *L'Esprit
du temps* (Moravia: Paris, 1989).

and his Ballets Russes. Cocteau: "Sun … I am black inside and rose outside."[1] Matisse, Picasso, Braque and Mondrian, his eternal guides. Joys and colours in the light of Marrakech. The sublimity and deliquescence of dying worlds along the "Guermantes Way" and in Visconti. The black veils of Maldoror and so many divas and queens, real or imagined, sisters of Emma Bovary, Hollywood goddesses and Maria Callas, who bestowed something of their secret selves on Saint Laurent's women.

When some of these ghosts began to make their mark, and the scenario he was looking for started to take shape, uncertain and fragile, the model and fabrics now entered the fray with the couturier for an amorous flirtation that was also a merciless duel between the "tender, the refined, the poetic" and "the barbarous, the wild"[2]; between the model's inspiring movements and the story that the couturier was beginning to write, between material and light. This dialogue is moving, threefold and simultaneous: between the couturier and the fabric, the mannequin and the model, and the couturier and

1. Extract from a poem by Jean Cocteau "Batterie" (1920), embroidered on a pink satin overcoat, autumn-winter 1980 haute couture collection.
2. Text written by Yves Saint Laurent on headed notepaper from 55 Rue de Babylone Paris 7.

his mannequin. A silent bodily engagement that is sometimes stubborn yet always cooperative, with the author and his theatrical performer speaking to each other of the gaze through the impartial intermediary of the all-seeing mirror. All Saint Laurent's *mannequins cabine* liked to "push" a garment so that the image would be perfect and the narrative evident. "I could write the story of my fashion with the names of my favourite models. ... Without my models," Saint Laurent never stopped repeating, "I might never have been able to discover the elegance of a body."[1] A body elevated to the status of an idol, at the heart of Saint Laurent's creation. He seized hold of his fantasies, and subjected them to his savoir faire and tamed them for a woman's body. "Sometimes there is a big fight within me between these fantasies and this woman's body whose rule is that I respect it. It is always the Woman's Body that triumphs, that wins. My deep truth is the humility of my ideas before the Reality of a Woman's body."[2]

This constant immolation of a limitless imagination on the altar of the woman

1. Text written by Yves Saint Laurent on headed notepaper from 55 Rue de Babylone Paris 7.
2. Ibid.

as idol is the exacting ascesis that created Saint Laurent. It enabled him to create an oeuvre by conquering a style, and to insert himself with his anxieties in heart-rending, couture-cut self-portrait. Did this born depressive unconsciously choose fashion as a Pascalian divertissement to offset his suffering, or did he deliberately choose his suffering as the foundations of his fashion? We think of Proust's words about the composer Vinteuil, which was long posted behind the couturier's desk at Avenue Marceau: "From what depths of what sorrows had he drawn that godlike strength, that unlimited power to create?"[1]

"Madeleine Renaud put it very nicely by saying that when you dressed a body, you made its soul visible. I would say, in turn, that when you create a dress you make your soul visible. And it is very beautiful, Yves Saint Laurent's soul, when it is displayed in the collections."[2] So, one festive evening, said Pierre Bergé, he who always carried on his shoulders the clouds on which Yves Saint Laurent, in his studio, travelled higher and higher, more and more solitarily. "Tonight,

1. Marcel Proust, *Du côté de chez Swann*, 1913.
2. Speech by Pierre Bergé during a party at the Lido celebrating twenty years of the Maison Saint Laurent, 28 January 1982.

you are going to create. Tonight, you will create. Tonight, you are creating."[1]

1. Allusion to Yves Saint Laurent's last words of adieu to La Callas: "Tonight you are going to sing. Tonight you will sing. Tonight you are singing." "La fin d'un rêve", *Le Monde*, 18-19 September 1977.

Author's note: all the handwritten texts by Yves Saint Laurent are archived at the Fondation Pierre Bergé - Yves Saint Laurent.

"It is a profession in which you are not free. You can make a very beautiful drawing and it may be betrayed. By the *première d'atelier*, by the model or by the fabric."

Rue Spontini, 1964. Yves Saint Laurent drawing at his worktable.
Photograph Marc Riboud

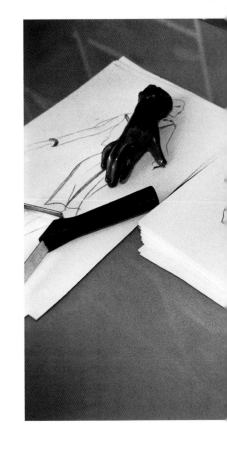

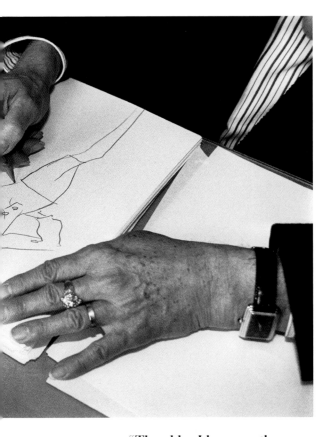

"The older I become, the more spontaneous [my sketches] are. I don't draw a dress precisely – it is always in movement. I have a better understanding of a woman's body now. It becomes almost an obsession. The body takes on such an importance, even more than the dress."

Magic hands to tell the story of Saint Laurent. 1991.
In the studio at 5 Avenue Marceau.
Photograph Martine Archambault

"I wanted to get back
to true femininity
by accumulating the
finery and ornaments
that have helped
feminine charm
through the ages."

Yves Saint Laurent
to Catherine Deneuve,
congratulating him after a show

Sketch for the "Spaniards" spring-summer 1977 haute couture collection.
No. 73: evening dress. Blouse and shawl in printed chiffon,
skirt in purple moiré ottoman. Petticoat in Bordeaux taffeta.

"The greatest change came
when I discovered my own
style without being influenced
by others. It was with
'le smoking' and the
transparent blouse. That is
when I became conscious of
the body. That is when I began
a dialogue with women
and began to understand better
what a modern woman is."

Sketch from the "bible", the working file created for each collection,
containing reproductions of sketches of models with details of fabrics,
accessories and suppliers. Tuxedo-Bermudas in alpaca and blouse in black
cigaline worn by Danielle. Spring-summer 1968 haute couture collection.

Jacket, trousers in striped grey gabardine, blouse in pink organdie and navy-blue tie. Between "Secrecy and Lust", a foretaste of the famous photograph by Helmut Newton, Rue Aubriot. From the "bible" of the spring-summer 1967 haute couture collection.

4109
Esther
Danielle
mousseline
noire.

Sketch of the famous dress in chiffon with moiré ostrich feathers, "flounced" by Danielle. Around the waist, a gold snake belt. Autumn-winter 1968 haute couture collection. Atelier: Madame Esther.

"Black veils always come back in my collections, it's the idea of death – when a collection is over, it doesn't belong to me anymore, and I die a little with it. The idea of veils of black chiffon or black tulle is almost a physical presence with me. It's mystery …"

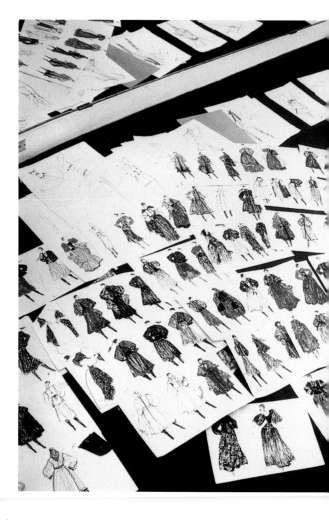

"It's an egotistical collection.
I put in it all I had in me, all my favourite
painters – Vermeer, Delacroix, Ingres,
La Tour, Rembrandt.
Then there is the theatrical side …
Then I put in my favorite heroines, like
Madame Bovary and Catherine of Russia."

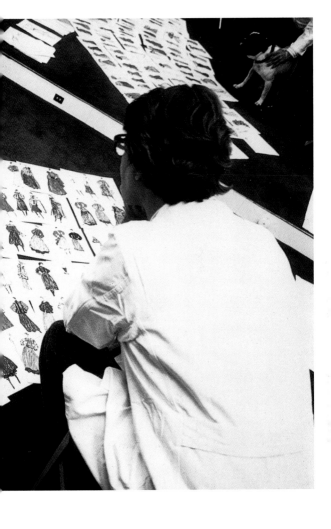

1983: Yves Saint Laurent in front of the 106 drawings of the "Opera-Ballets Russes" autumn-winter 1976 haute couture collection, for the catalogue of the exhibition at the Metropolitan Museum.
Photograph Duane Michals

"I couldn't live without
my gypsy atmosphere –
the books, the magazines,
the papers, the postcards,
the enormous disorder…
I hate a room that looks
deserted and sanctified.
I like a room to be completely
anonymous, like a hotel
room, or a reflection of a
person's most intimate life."

Yves Saint Laurent pinning sketches on the wall of his studio
at 5 Avenue Marceau, described by Anthony Burgess
as "marvellously cluttered". 1982.
Photograph Pierre Boulat

"Pierre Bergé, the last chance."

Rue Jean-Goujon, December 1961.
A legend, "YSL", is about to be born.
Yves Saint Laurent and Pierre Bergé.
Photograph Pierre Boulat

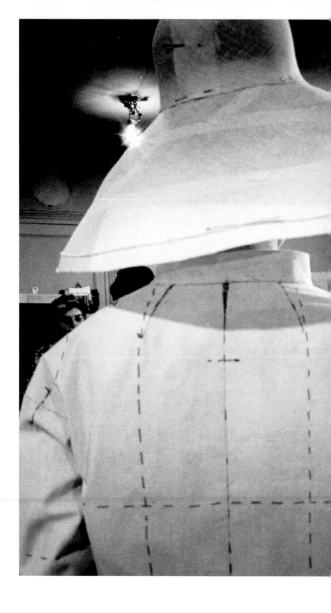

"I am an artisan. Haute couture is a great profession, with secrets whispered between initiates."

YSL judging a toile for his first collection.
Rue Jean-Goujon, January 1962.
Photograph Pierre Boulat

"The poet of fashion" and "the little princess of high taste taught by Paul Valéry and Rainer Maria Rilke", as Lucien François might have said. An amused Saint Laurent and Victoire, his favourite model, enjoy the possibilities of a panoply of toiles. Rue Jean-Goujon, January 1962.
Photograph Pierre Boulat

"It was a big room … The place was splendidly chaotic. No director could ever have created one with such wit and imagination. White veils on the windows, samples of fabrics and embroideries, of buttons and braiding hanging from the walls or forming huge piles on the floor, sketches of costumes that Saint Laurent designed for Roland Petit, … a photo of Christian Dior, just behind the desk of the charming gazelle in glasses …"

Dino Buzzati

The original team in Saint Laurent's first studio in Rue Jean-Goujon.
From left, Gabrielle Busschaert (press attaché), Victoire, Claude Licard
(assistant to Monsieur Saint Laurent), Madame Esther (*première d'atelier*),
Pierre Bergé (behind the couturier), Robert Herscovici and the model Heather.
Photograph Pierre Boulat

1

"The wonderful
thing about
this profession
is that dream and
reality are one.
From the Dream,
Reality is only
a step away."

In the end, this dream of a toile pinned with a multicoloured flight of butterflies, a pattern for later embroidery, did not make YSL's final haute collection, for spring-summer 2002.

Photograph Alexandra Boulat

"Going deeper into my craft is so fascinating. I know nothing more exciting than that. You think that everything has stopped for good, is set in stone, and then suddenly you see depths, glints of light that you thought were out of reach, and that you come to understand and appreciate better as the experience grows richer."

Fitting a toile from the autumn-winter 1977
haute couture collection on the model Kirat.
Photograph André Perlstein

"Couture means endless patience.
You can't strive for perfection
and at the same time aim for novelty.
I know where I stand. My ambition
is not to surprise, to give frissons,
but to provide women with
a few basic garments that they can
count on."

Yves Saint Laurent in his studio on Avenue Marceau in 1982.
Photograph Pierre Boulat

"It's difficult you know,
recapturing your
naivety after all those
years in the business."

Fitting a toile in 1992.
Photograph Pierre Boulat

"It's wrong to mistrust one's sensibility. It is the richest, finest and most effective thing we have for understanding people and things."

The studio, Avenue Marceau, 1982. A model, a toile, sketches
scattered over the floor: Yves Saint Laurent deep in thought and
Moujik, faithful watcher of his master's thoughts.
Photograph Pierre Boulat

"I see myself as an
intellectual artist rather
than an experimental
sociologist."

Elle, 14 September 1967: "Yves Saint Laurent
is the champion of black. He works in a white cotton
coat in Forain's former studio. On the table,
neatly ordered knickknacks, a telephone
and his famous glasses."
Photograph Jean Hubert

"Haute couture is material, it's also a whisper that is passed on and repeated. We whisper our secrets. That is where haute couture can become a kind of art."

Yves Saint Laurent in 1977 with his battery of fabric rolls.
Photograph André Perlstein

"If he has a religion, its deity is without doubt woman."

Anthony Burgess

Yves Saint Laurent inventing a dress for
the 1977 autumn-winter haute couture collection on the "goddess" Kirat.
Photograph André Perlstein

"You know what Proust
said, about the artist
not being interested in
anything but his own
work. If you allow that
my work is my destiny,
then my attitude is quite
understandable."

Self-portrait, spring 1975. Yves Saint Laurent poses
for *Vogue Hommes*. Is it the negative of the man or of
his work?
Photograph Uli Rose

"I like to see a model move in my clothes, the way she brings them to life or, if they aren't right or final, the way she rejects them. A good model can bring fashion forward ten years."

In the studio in Rue Spontini, Yves Saint Laurent draping Danielle – "a very long neck and superb shoulders" – in 3.8 metres of crêpe with a green, black and white print by Abraham for the spring-summer 1969 haute couture collection. Behind the model, the *première d'atelier*, Mademoiselle Blanche.
Photograph Claude Azoulay

"Monsieur Saint Laurent would
love to dress Scarlett O'Hara,
the Duchesse de Guermantes,
Anna Karenina, the Traviata,
Emma Bovary, Scheherazade,
Phaedra, Bérénice."

Pierre Bergé

The couturier at work in 1976, inspired perhaps
by a Marlene Dietrich lookalike.
Photograph Guy Marineau

"With people of talent,
those with whom
I surround myself in both
my working and personal
life, talk is rarely necessary.
There is a telepathy
that goes beyond words,
a complicity of intent,
an understanding."

1982. In the studio on Avenue Marceau, Yves Saint Laurent,
Loulou de La Falaise and Anne-Marie Muñoz, studio director,
concentrating on the mirror as they judge the effect of a fabric.
Photograph Pierre Boulat

"I'm thrilled like a child to feel that after fifteen years of struggle, angst and terror I have a grip on this craft that was always running ahead of me. Now I am holding it tight and I'll never let it fly away again. The fabric flows naturally on the body and nobody knows what agonies I went through to attain this naturalness, this lightness."

Eyes glued to the studio mirror, Anne-Marie Muñoz, Monsieur Jean-Pierre, *premier d'atelier Tailleur*, a model, Madame Ida, head of the workshops and Monsieur Saint Laurent. Communion and Love … The "Chinese" autumn-winter 1977 haute couture collection.

Photograph André Perlstein

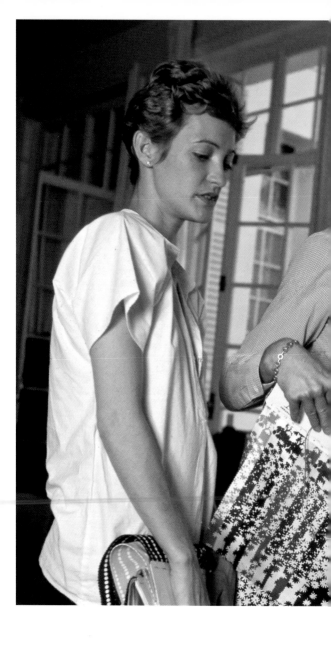

The studio on Avenue Marceau, 1975. Yves Saint Laurent and Loulou de La Falaise working on the spring-summer 1976 *rive gauche* collection.
Photograph Robert Alan Clayton

"I can't explain [Loulou's] job … it has to do with her manner, her straightforwardness. I trust her reactions. She is a sounding board for my ideas. I bounce thoughts off her and they come back more clear. She has great taste and a feeling for what is right … and she is a woman."

"The anxiety isn't all the questions about the position of the pockets, the belt or the form, the anxiety is when you are dealing with the fabric and the colour. You have to tame the material so that the dress comes out the way you imagined it."

1975. Yves Saint Laurent with Christian Dior's cane, accompanied by his two vestals, Loulou de La Falaise (left) and Anne-Marie Muñoz (to the rear), with studio assistant Jean-Louis Moncé. Fabric matters.
Photograph Robert Alan Clayton

"Pierre Bergé acts as my ramparts,
my protection, fending off bad elements
and seeing things through."

1977, the agonies of preparing a collection.
Loulou de La Falaise and Pierre Bergé.
Photograph André Perlstein

"If you hadn't been
Yves Saint Laurent,
who would you have
wanted to be?
— Picasso, Marcel
Proust, Matisse, or
all three."

In the studio in 1986, Yves Saint Laurent pointing to a detail of his collection
boards with Christian Dior's cane.

D. R.

"Without my models
I might never have
discovered the secret
elegance of a body.
Whenever I work with
them I am moved by
the length of a neck,
the ideal swaying of
the shoulders, the line
of the back, the curve
of a bust, the
harmonious gait of a
leg, the moving secrets
of a woman's body."

September 1987. Observed by Lord Snowdon for *Vogue UK*,
Yves Saint Laurent and Katoucha in a black velvet skirt with a violet taffeta
flounce for the *rive gauche* collection.

15

"I try to capture a bodily posture and,
in the end, a moral posture: a woman's liberty
and responsiveness. This comes from
observing people I know, that I go out with,
and others I don't know, girls I see living
their lives, who impose their tastes and ideas,
who influence me."

1 February 1969. For *Paris Match*, Yves Saint Laurent
opens the door to his studio in Rue Spontini
and reveals the bomb he is about to drop into the world
of fashion: the dress 25 centimetres from the
floor – a real new look in the age of the miniskirt.
The dress is to be worn without jewellery or bra.
Photograph Claude Azoulay

"My imaginary museum?
The Pagodenburg in
Munich, the salon of the
Vicomte and Vicomtesse
de Noailles by Jean-Michel
Frank, *The Turkish Bath*
by Ingres, the Burne-
Jones in the Metropolitan
Museum, New York,
the manuscript of *À la
recherche du temps perdu*
and Shanghai Express by
Josef von Sternberg."

With Nicole in Rue Spontini, the last fitting of a model for the autumn-winter 1973 haute couture collection. Leather short coat with fox-fur edging, brown flannel trousers with a snake-head gold chain belt and tie-front blouse.

Photograph Marc Riboud

"Like Scott F. Fitzgerald, I love decadent frenzy. I love Visconti. I saw the balls of the 1950s. The splendour of powerful haute couture. I knew the youth of the 1960s: Talitha and Paul Getty, beautiful and damned, and a whole generation brought together, as if for eternity, where the curtain of the past seemed to be rising on to an extraordinary future."

Loulou de La Falaise, Yves Saint Laurent and glints
of transparency and gold on the model Willy van Rooy
during a final fitting for the "Opera-Ballets Russes"
autumn-winter 1976 haute couture collection.
Photograph Jeanloup Sieff

"At last, I am entering the secrets
of the Imperial City and from there
I am freeing you, my aesthetic ghosts,
my queens, my divas, my festive
whirlwinds, my nights of ink and crêpe
de Chine, my Coromandel lacquers, my
artificial lakes, my hanging gardens."

July 1977, in the studio on Avenue Marceau,
Yves Saint Laurent puts a finishing touch to a model
for the "Chinese" haute couture collection shortly before the show.
23   Photograph Guy Marineau

"My idea of a woman is an object of worship, and I'm thinking not only in the holy sense, but also as something to be covered with gold, the way the Conquistadors adorned statues of the Virgin with booty – covering her with gold and presents."

Yves Saint Laurent accessorizing with a profusion of gold
and jewels the "Homage to William Shakespeare" wedding dress/idol to be worn
by Mounia in the autumn-winter 1980 haute couture show.
Photograph François-Marie Banier

"When I am working my mind is set on paring things down, more and more. Perhaps, at the end, there'll be nothing left. ... I would like to reach the point where people can say: it is nothing, and it is everything."

This confidence vouchsafed in 1986 announces the draped garments of
Saint Laurent's last collection in January 2002: the unique evanescence
of a chiffon by Bianchini-Férier for a liquid architecture, the climax
of Saint Laurent's Oeuvre. The model Amalia (from the back), Loulou
de La Falaise and Yves Saint Laurent.
Photograph Alexandra Boulat

POSTFACE

Yves Saint Laurent's studio on Avenue Marceau was reduced to its simplest and most noble form. Intimate, secret in its proportions, one side was covered by the traditional wall of the fitting mirror where the couturier would ritually judge the proportions and movements of his models by studying their reflection.

At the centre stood the work table heaped with sketches. A wooden board and two trestles, no other artifice. Saint Laurent's office is like a student's, the metaphor for his eternal youth, a wealth of nothing to achieve such great things.

Hedi Slimane

Yves Saint Laurent's studio by Hedi Slimane, November 2008.

vert
plus
froid

+ Blanc

Les vert
les Bleus gris
Les marrons absol

Tout dans les
verts particu
liers

vert
jaune
lumi
neux

"What trace would you like to leave?
That of an artist who created an oeuvre
or that of a magician of the ephemeral?
— **An artist who created an oeuvre.**
— Is it important for you to go down
in posterity?
— **Yes, I would love it if in a hundred
years time people studied my dresses,
my drawings. There are already plans
for a Fondation Yves Saint Laurent,
with all my work, after my death.
I hope that won't be too soon …**"

The Fondation Pierre Bergé - Yves Saint Laurent, which opened in 2004, is founded on forty years of creativity. Recognized as a public utility, it has three missions:

The rigorous museological conservation of a unique heritage comprising five thousand haute couture garments and fifteen thousand accessories, as well as thousands of sketches, collection boards, photographs and objects.

The organization of exhibitions, both in the refurbished spaces at 5 Avenue Marceau and in museums around the world, promoting Yves Saint Laurent's work.

Support for cultural institutions that encourage contemporary arts.

In 2011, the Fondation Pierre Bergé - Yves Saint Laurent decided to open its most secret spaces to the public. The former haute couture salons and Yves Saint Laurent's studio are now accessible via a guided tour that tells the story of the couture house and reveals the creative process behind the collections.

For more information:
www.fondation-pb-ysl.net

Drawing of Yves Saint Laurent's studio by Uli Gassmann, June 2009.

Acknowledgements

Pierre Bergé warmly thanks all those who contributed to the making of this book:
Jéromine Savignon, Hedi Slimane and Yann Rzepka, Uli and Gay Gassmann.
He also thanks:
Jean-Paul Capitani, Anne-Sylvie Bameule, Raphaëlle Pinoncély, Marie-Amélie Le Roy, Aïté Bresson and Mencia Morère at Éditions Actes Sud.
Olivier Gabet, Chantal Lachkar, Lysiane Allinieu, Carole Balut and Emmanuelle Beuvin at the Arts Décoratifs; the Palais Galliera, Musée de la Mode de la Ville de Paris; Philippe Le Moult.
Philippe Mugnier, Olivier Flaviano, Laetitia Roux, Pauline Vidal, Simon Freschard, Alice Coulon, Sandrine Tinturier, Catherine Gadala, Catherine Zeitoun, Laurence Neveu, Angela Krieger, Pascal Sittler and everyone at the Fondation Pierre Bergé - Yves Saint Laurent.

Jéromine Savignon thanks Pierre Bergé from the bottom of her heart for offering her, with such sensitivity, the keys to the studio of Yves Saint Laurent and to the secrets of his mirror.
She also thanks Hedi Slimane for the gift of his postface and his photographs, which are so beautiful, so moving, so emotionally in tune with Saint Laurent, and the Fondation Pierre Bergé - Yves Saint Laurent and Éditions Actes Sud.
She also thanks all those who, in different ways, were so helpful to her in writing this book: Mage Barbier, Ilaria Borrelli, Corinne Buscaylet, Gabrielle Busschaert, Emmanuelle Beuvin, Madison Cox, Charlotte Deffe, Jean-Pierre Derbord, Dominique Deroche, Victoire Doutreleau, Uli and Gay Gassmann, Mary Jim Josephs, Xavier Landrit, Marie-José Lepicard, Laïla Marrakchi, Vincent Mermier, Cristina Romero, Violeta Sanchez, Bernard Savignon, David Teboul, Dominique Thomas, Pierre Thoretton, Élie Top, Susan Train and Connie Uzzo.
And finally, she dedicates this book to her son, Ludwig.

Quotes

Page 4: Anthony Burgess, *The New York Times Magazine*, 11 September 1977 / Page 11: Jean Cocteau, *L'Album du Figaro*, February- March 1950 / Page 13: Preparatory text by Yves Saint Laurent for the exhibition catalogue "Yves Saint Laurent" at the Costume Institute of the Metropolitan Museum, 22 July 1983 / Page 61: Yves Saint Laurent, *Elle*, 23 September 1967 / Page 63: Yves Saint Laurent, *Women's Wear Daily*, 24 April 1978 / Page 64: Yves Saint Laurent, *France-Soir*, 28 January 1977 / Page 66: Yves Saint Laurent, *Newsweek*, 18 November 1974 / Page 69: Yves Saint Laurent, *Vogue US*, December 1983 / Page 70: Yves Saint Laurent, *Time*, 16 August 1976 / Page 72: Yves Saint Laurent, *Women's Wear Daily*, 24 April 1978 / Page 76: Yves Saint Laurent, *20 ans*, April 1973 / Page 80: Dino Buzzati, *Corriere della Sera*, 30 January 1962 / Page 82: handwritten text by Yves Saint Laurent, February 1991 / Page 84: Preparatory text by Yves Saint Laurent for the exhibition catalogue "Yves Saint Laurent" at the Costume Institute of the Metropolitan Museum, 22 July 1983 / Page 86: Yves Saint Laurent, *GAP*, September 1974 / Page 88: Yves Saint Laurent, *GAP*, September 1974 / Page 90: Handwritten text by Yves Saint Laurent, undated / Page 92: Yves Saint Laurent, *The Sunday Telegraph*, 17 July 1966 / Page 94: Yves Saint Laurent, *Le Monde*, 8 December 1983 / Page 96: Anthony Burgess, *The New York Times Magazine*, 11 September 1977 / Page 98: Yves Saint Laurent, *Le Figaro*, 15 July 1991 / Page 100: Preparatory text by Yves Saint Laurent for the exhibition catalogue "Yves Saint Laurent" at the Costume Institute of the Metropolitan Museum, 22 July 1983 / Page 102: Pierre Bergé, note from the Maison Yves Saint Laurent, November 1983 / Page 104: Yves Saint Laurent, *Vogue US*, November 1972 / Page 106: Yves Saint Laurent, mid–1970s / Page 109: Yves Saint Laurent, *Vogue US*, November 1972 / Page 110: Yves Saint Laurent, *Le Monde*, 8 December 1983 / Page 111: Yves Saint Laurent, *Vogue US*, November 1972 / Page 112: Undated answer to questions from the *Corriere della Sera* / Page 114: Handwritten text by Yves Saint Laurent, undated / Page 116: Yves Saint Laurent, *Le Journal du dimanche*, 2 February 1969 / Page 118: Yves Saint Laurent, *L'Express*, July 1973 / Page 120: Preparatory text by Yves Saint Laurent for the exhibition catalogue "Yves Saint Laurent" at the Costume Institute of the Metropolitan Museum, 22 July 1983 / Page 122: Text by Yves Saint Laurent about his "Chinese" haute couture collection, autumn-winter 1977, for a book project (unpublished) / Page 124: Yves Saint Laurent, *Vogue US*, December 1983 / Page 126: Yves Saint Laurent, *Libération*, 31 May 1986 / Page 137: Jean-Dominique Bauby and Francine Vormèse, "Saint Laurent: 30 ans de passion", *Elle*, 27 January 1992.

Photographic credits

Cover and p. 132–33: © Hedi Slimane / pp. 5, 85, 97, 106–07, 111: © André Perlstein / pp. 12–13, 73, 74–75, 76–77, 78–79, 80–81, 86–87, 88–89, 91, 104–05: © Pierre Boulat courtesy Association Pierre et Alexandra Boulat / pp. 61, 119: © Marc Riboud / p. 63: © Martine Archambault - Figarophoto / pp. 70–71: © The Metropolitan Museum of Art - Photograph by Duane Michals / pp. 82–83, 126–27: © Alexandra Boulat courtesy Association Pierre et Alexandra Boulat / pp. 92–93: © Jean Hubert - *Elle* - Scoop / p. 95: © André Perlstein, www.andre-perlstein.com - Camerapress - Gamma / pp. 98–99: © Uli Rose - *Vogue Paris* / pp. 101, 116–17: © Claude Azoulay - *Paris Match* / pp. 102–03, 122–23: © Guy Marineau / pp. 108–09, 110: © Robert Alan Clayton / pp. 112–13: DR / pp. 114–15: photograph Lord Snowdon © Armstrong Jones / pp. 120–21: © The Estate of Jeanloup Sieff / p. 125: © François-Marie Banier.

Graphic design: Raphaëlle Pinoncély
Translation: Charles Penwarden
Copy editing: Bronwyn Mahoney
Production: Camille desproges
Photoengraving: Terre Neuve

Printed November 2019
by Graphius, Gent, Belgium
for Actes Sud,
Le Méjan, Place Nina-Berberova, 13200 Arles.

Legal deposit: September 2014